How to Raise and Train a

DACHSHUND

By LOIS MEISTRELL

and SARA M. BARBARESI

Distributed in the U.S.A. by T.F.H. Publications, Inc., 211 West Sylvania Avenue, P.O. Box 27, Neptune City, N.J. 07753; in England by T.F.H. (Gt. Britain) Ltd., 13 Nutley Lane, Reigate, Surrey; in Canada to the book store and library trade by Clarke, Irwin & Company, Clarwin House, 791 St. Clair Avenue West, Toronto 10, Ontario; in Canada to the pet trade by Rolf C. Hagen Ltd., 3225 Sartelon Street, Montreal 382, Quebec; in Southeast Asia by Y.W. Ong, 9 Lorong 36 Geylang, Singapore 14; in Australia and the south Pacific by Pet Imports Pty. Ltd., P.O. Box 149, Brookvale 2100, N.S.W., Australia. Published by T.F.H. Publications, Inc. Ltd., The British Crown Colony of Hong Kong.

DEDICATION

The authors would like to dedicate this book to the memory of the late Josef Mehrer, who did so much to promote the welfare of the Dachshund in America.

PHOTOS BY AL BARRY from THREE LIONS, Inc.

Pictures taken with the cooperation of Great Neck Dog Training Center, Mr. and Mrs. Harland Meistrell, L.I., N.Y.; Miss E. S. Bromley, Philadelphia, Pa.; Mrs. Vera Jackson, Millbrook Kennels, Solebury, Pa.; Mrs. Josef Mehrer, Marienlust Kennels, W. Hempstead, L.I. and Mr. and Mrs. Frank Hardy, East Meadow, L.I., N.Y.

ISBN 0-87666-276-9

Manufactured in the United States of America

Library of Congress Catalog Card No. 58-7599

Contents

The Dachshund is a member of the Hound group of breeds, though most of the 200,000 that have been registered in the United States in the past ten years are house pets rather than field dogs.

1. Dachshund Standards

Of the one hundred and more breeds of dogs in the United States today, probably the most distinctive is the Dachshund. With its short legs and long body, the Dachshund has often been caricatured, but it is loved and admired by many, so many, in fact, that the breed has risen in popularity to second-ranking of all purebreds.

The Dachshund is a member of the Hound group of breeds, although its name in German (properly pronounced "Dox-hoont") means "badger dog," not "hound." In Europe the Dachshund has been used for centuries to hunt the rabbit and the badger, a small but ferocious cousin of the mole and skunk, and was developed specifically for this sport. Short, easily folded legs, a long body with plenty of breathing capacity and elastic skin were useful qualities for a dog built to hunt in narrow, twisting burrows. The long head with powerful jaw was selectively bred to fight its prey. Even a long, strong tail comes in handy when the hunting dog must be forcibly removed backward from a dead-end burrow.

Although most of the 200,000 Dachshunds registered in the last ten years are house pets, not hunters or working dogs, this small but hardy breed is no pampered darling. The courage and determination bred into badger dogs remain in the independent and often stubborn Dachshund which makes its home with, and readily adopts, your family. An individualist, yes, but not willfully disobedient or hard to train, the Dachshund is clever and quick at learning and can be a charming and enjoyable companion, especially when properly trained.

Dachshunds are clean little dogs, and have no doggy odor. They need little in the way of grooming, although an occasional brushing will take care of loose hair and prevent it from becoming a nuisance on the furniture. Because of their small size and neat ways, they make excellent dogs for city apartments, but are also at home in the country and can adapt to an unheated outdoor doghouse, provided it is snugly built.

HISTORY OF THE BREED

It has been claimed that the Dachshund goes back to 2000 B.C. and one of its kind was painted on an Egyptian monument. Earliest modern records show that the Dachshund, often referred to as the Teckel or Dackel

5

Dachshunds are recognized in three coats: From left to right, the smooth or short-haired, the wire-haired and the long-haired.

also, was first called by its current name in the 16th and 17th centuries. The breed has been developed along the same lines since that time. For a while two breeds, one a hound and the other a terrier type were bred. Today, there are three varieties, of which the Smooth is best known, although the elegant Long-haired is gaining favor, and the Wire-haired Dachshund is more often seen and less of a curiosity these days. Size has gradually been reduced so that Standards are under thirty pounds, usually around twenty, while the Miniature, which also appears in all three coat varieties, is under nine pounds.

The Dachshund is popular all over the world. It is the leading breed in Austria and Sweden as well as in its native Germany, and among the top ten most popular dogs in most European countries. As early as 1840, Dachshunds were registered in a stud book, and a breed club was founded in 1888. There was also a hunting Dachshund association which recorded dogs of proven hunting achievement and conducted field trials. The first Dachshunds imported into the United States were pets, however, and only recently has there been a revival of interest in hunting. The Dachshund Club of America, founded in 1895, sponsors a field trial in addition to show and obedience activities. Dachshunds in the three varieties, now judged separately, often form the largest entry of any breed at dog shows, including the nation's most famous, the Westminster,

Dachshunds come in a variety of colors, of which red, varying from tan to liver, is the most common, followed by black-and-tan. Equally acceptable are chocolate or gray with tan markings over the eyes, around the mouth and on the legs and underpart of the body and tail. Dapple and brindle are also attractive recognized colors.

SUMMARY OF DACHSHUND STANDARD

A brief summary of the Dachshund standard follows. The complete standard may be obtained from the secretary of the Dachshund Club of America, Mrs. William Burr Hill, West John Street, Hicksville, L.I., N.Y., or obtained from the American Kennel Club, 221 Fourth Ave., New York 3, N.Y.

GENERAL APPEARANCE: Short-legged, long-bodied, low-to-ground; sturdy, well-muscled, neither clumsy nor slim, with audacious carriage and intelligent expression; conformation pre-eminently fitted for following game into burrows.

HEAD: Long, uniformly tapered, clean-cut; teeth well fitted, with scissor bite; eyes medium oval; ears broad, long, rounded, set on high and well back; neck long, muscular.

A long, uniformly sloping head with long, broad ears makes the profile of a Dachshund very distinctive and attractive.

FOREQUARTERS: Muscular, compact. Chest deep, long, full and oval; breastbone prominent. Broad, long shoulder and oblique humerus forming right angle; heavy, set close; forearm short, inclined slightly in. Foreleg straight and vertical in profile, covering deepest point of chest. Feet broad, firm, compact, turned slightly out.

HINDQUARTERS: Well-muscled and rounded. Pelvis, tibia and femur oblique, forming right angles; tarsus inclined forward. Hip should be level with shoulder, back strong, neither sagged nor more than very slightly arched. Tail strong, well tapered, well covered with hair, not carried gaily.

VARIETIES: Three coat types: SMOOTH or Short-haired, short and dense, shining, glossy. WIRE-HAIRED, like German Spiky-haired Pointer, hard with good undercoat. LONG-HAIRED, like Irish Setter.

MINIATURE: Symmetrical, rather slender body conformation below maximum limits of 11.8 (female) and 13.8 inches chest girth; 7.7 and 8.8 pounds weight at minimum age of 12 months.

COLOR: Solid red (tan) of various shades, and black with tan points, should have black noses and tails, and narrow black line edging lips and eyelids; chocolate with tan points permits brown nose. Eyes of all lustrous, the darker the better.

FAULTS: Over- or under-shot, knuckling over, loose shoulders, high on legs, clumsy gait; long, splayed or twisted feet; sagged or roached back; high croup; small, narrow or short chest; faulty angulation of fore- or hindquarters; weak loins, narrow hindquarters, bowed legs, cowhocks, weak or dish-faced muzzle, dewlaps, uneven or scanty coats.

2. Buying Your Dachshund

Once you have decided that you want a Dachshund, the next thing to do is to go about getting him. Perhaps you chose the Dachshund because a neighbor's dog had puppies and the children talked you into it. If the pups are for sale, your task is an easy one. But more likely you just decided that the Dachshund was the dog for you, and now you have to find the right one.

First, make up your mind what you want: male or female, adult or puppy, show dog or "just a pet." There is no greater use for a dog than being "just" a beloved pet and companion, but the dog which has profitable show and breeding possibilities is worth more to the seller.

PET OR SHOW DOG?

The puppy with a slight flaw in the set of his ears or curve of his legs will make just as good a companion and guardian, but his more perfect litter mate will cost more.

That is why there is often a difference in price between puppies which look—to you, anyway—identical. If you think you may want to show your dog or raise a litter of puppies for the fun of it later on, by all means buy the best you can afford. You will save expense and disappointment later on. However, if the puppy is *strictly* a pet for the children, or companion for you, you can afford to look for a bargain. The pup which is not show material; the older pup, for which there is often less demand; or the grown dog, not up to being used for breeding, are occasionally available and are opportunities to save money. Remember that these are the only real bargains in buying a dog. It takes good food and care—and plenty of both—to raise a healthy, vigorous puppy.

The price you pay for your dog is little compared to the love and devotion he will return over the many years he'll be with you. With good care and affection your pup should live to a ripe old age; through modern veterinary science and nutrition, dogs are better cared for and living longer. Their average life expectancy is now eight or nine years, and dogs in their teens are not uncommon.

A Dachshund is one of the few breeds that man doesn't try to improve with a knife or scissors. The tail is not cut nor are the ears trimmed. The puppy is essentially the same as the mother.

MALE OR FEMALE?

If you should intend breeding your dog in the future, by all means buy a female. You can find a suitable mate without difficulty when the time comes, and have the pleasure of raising a litter of pups—there is nothing cuter than a fat, playful puppy. If you don't want to raise puppies, your female can be spayed, and will remain a healthy, lively pet. The female is smaller than the male and generally quieter. She has less tendency to roam in search of romance, but a properly trained male can be a charming pet, and has a certain difference in temperament that is appealing to many people. Male vs. female is chiefly a matter of personal choice.

ADULT OR PUP?

Whether to buy a grown dog or a small puppy is another question. It is undeniably fun to watch your dog grow all the way from a baby, sprawling and playful, to a mature, dignified dog. If you don't have the time to spend on the more frequent meals, housebreaking, and other training a puppy needs in order to become a dog you can be proud of, then choose an older, partly trained pup or a grown dog. If you want a show dog, remember that no one, not even an expert, can predict with 100% accuracy what a small puppy will be when he grows up. He may be right *most* of the time, but six months is the earliest age for the would-be exhibitor to pick a prospect and know that his future is relatively safe.

If you have a small child it is best to get a puppy big enough to defend himself, one not less than four or five months old. Older children will enjoy playing with and helping to take care of a baby pup, but at less than four months a puppy wants to do little but eat and sleep, and he must be protected from teasing and overtiring. You cannot expect a very young child to understand that a puppy is a fragile living being; to the youngster he is a toy like his stuffed dog.

WHERE TO BUY

You can choose among several places to buy your dog. One is a kennel which breeds show dogs as a business and has extra pups for sale as pets. Another is the one-dog owner who wants to sell the puppies from an occasional litter, paying for the expenses being his chief aim. Pet shops usually buy puppies from overstocked kennels or part-time hobbyists for re-sale, and you can generally buy a puppy there at a reasonable price. To find any of these, watch the pet column of your local newspaper or look in the classified section of your phone book. If you or your friends go driving out in the countryside, be on the lookout for a sign announcing pure-bred puppies for sale.

Whichever source you try, you can usually tell in a very short time whether the puppies will make healthy and happy pets. If they are clean, fat and lively, they are probably in good health. At the breeder's you will have the advantage of seeing the puppies' mother and perhaps the father and other relatives. Remember that the mother, having just raised a demanding family, won't be looking her best, but if she is sturdy, friendly and well-mannered, her puppies should be, too. If you feel that something is lacking in the care or condition of the dogs, it is better to look elsewhere than to buy hastily and regret it afterward.

You may be impatient to bring your dog home, but a few days will make little difference in its long and happy life with you, and it is better not to bring it into your home until it is prepared for the pup's arrival. A deposit will hold him for several days or a week. For instance, the Christmas puppy should be settled into his new home before the holidays or else wait until the excitement has died down. You may want to wait until the puppy's immunization shots have been completed, and if this is arranged in advance it is generally agreeable.

If you cannot find the dog you want locally, write to the secretary of the Dachshund Club or to the A.K.C. (see page 7) for names of breeders near you or to whom you can write for information. In this day of air travel, puppies are often bought by mail from reputable breeders.

WHAT TO LOOK FOR IN A PUPPY

In choosing your puppy, assuming that it comes from healthy, well-bred parents, look for one that is friendly and out-going. The biggest pup in the litter is apt to be somewhat coarse as a grown dog, while the appealing "poor little runt" may turn out to be a timid shadow—or have a Napoleon complex! If you want a show dog and have no experience in choosing the prospect, study the standard (page 7), but be advised by the breeder on the finer points of conformation. His prices will be in accord with the puppies' expected worth, and he will be honest with you because it is to his own advantage. He wants his good puppies placed in the public eye to reflect glory on him—and to attract future buyers.

If you are interested in showing your dog, it is a good idea to attend a dog show or two in your locale before buying your future entry. Watch the judging and ask exhibitors for information—some of them will probably have young stock for sale. For a list of coming dog shows write to the Gaines Dog Research Center, 250 Park Avenue, New York 17, N.Y.

The puppy should have a bright eye, without too much haw, or inner eyelid, showing in the corner. The head should be long, with dark eye, the body long, with well-sprung ribs. Short legs should be set well under the brisket, or chest, and the back should be neither sway nor roach (or arched). The tail should be long and tapered. In the Smooth, richness of coloring is desirable; the Long-haired should have a flat-lying coat with plenty of feathering on the legs and tail, and the hair on the ears should extend well below the tips. The puppy's coat should give promise of fulfilling these requirements. The Wire-haired's coat should be rough and hard.

Although the puppy may wobble clumsily when it moves, it should be able with coaxing to step out briskly and put one foot in front of the other instead of meandering or crossing in front of itself. The puppy should be lively and scamper with its littermates instead of sitting alone all the time.

Now that you have paid your money and made your choice, you are ready to depart with puppy, papers and instructions. Make sure that you know its feeding routine, and take along some of the same kind of food if you have not already bought some. It is best to make any changes in diet gradually so as not to upset digestion. If the puppy is not fed immediately before leaving, it should ride comfortably in your lap. Take along a towel or newspaper just in case, however.

PEDIGREES

When you buy your puppy you should receive its pedigree and registration certificate or application. These have nothing to do with licensing, which is a local ordinance applying to purebred and mongrel alike. Most puppies do not need to be licensed until they are six months old, but find out the local rule, buy a license when necessary, and keep it on your dog's

A pedigree and registration of a dog only testifies to his being a true representative of the breed. It has nothing to do with his being a good pet. Dachshunds are very gentle and make fine pets for children.

collar. An identification tag with your name, address and telephone number is also a good idea.

Your dog's pedigree is a chart showing its family tree, for your use and interest only; it is not part of his official papers. The registration certificate is the important part. If the dog was registered and named by his breeder, you will want to complete the transfer right away and send it with the fee of $1.00 to the American Kennel Club, 221 Fourth Ave., New York 3, N.Y.

Otherwise when you send in your transfer of ownership, you may insert a name of your own choosing on the application. Try to make it original, combining parents' names, which will often be German in origin, befitting the breed. To avoid having numerals attached because of duplication, i.e.,

Hansel XXV, call him Hansel von Schmidt, Hansel of Howardville, or something similar. You may combine your own names, the name of the village, street, or some other term which has a particular appeal to you. Regardless of registered name you may call the puppy by a shorter one, which is referred to as its "call" name.

Fill out the form carefully and mail it with the required fee of $2.00 to the A.K.C. Make sure that the number of the puppy's litter is included; you may have to wait to receive it from the breeder. The A.K.C. will record the dog in your name and send back your permanent certificate.

3. Care of the Dachshund Puppy

BRINGING YOUR PUPPY HOME

When you bring your puppy home, remember that he is used to the peace and relative calm of a life of sleeping, eating and playing with his brothers and sisters. The trip away from all this is an adventure in itself, and so is adapting to a new home. So let him take it easy for awhile. Don't let the whole neighborhood pat and poke him at one time. Be particularly careful when children want to handle him, for they cannot understand the difference between a delicate living puppy and the toy dog they play with and maul. If the puppy is to grow up loving children and taking care of them, he must not get a bad first impression.

THE PUPPY'S BED

It is up to you to decide where the puppy will sleep. Unless it is winter in a cold climate, even a young puppy can sleep outside in a snug, well-built dog house. It should have a tight, pitched roof to let the rain run off, and a floor off the ground, to avoid dampness. The door should be no larger than the grown dog will need to go in and out, as a bigger opening lets in too much draft. For bedding you can use an old rag or blanket, straw, or sweet-smelling cedar shavings. Whether the puppy sleeps indoors or out, he will benefit from an outdoor run of his own where he can be put to exercise and amuse himself. It does not have to be large for if he goes for walks and plays with you he will get enough exercise that way. He is much safer shut in his run than being left loose to follow a stray dog off your property and get into bad habits—if he isn't hit by a car first!

Of course if the dog is left in his run for any length of time he should have protection from the cold, rain or sun. The run should be rectangular, and as large as you can conveniently make it, up to 15 x 30 feet, with a strong wire fence to keep intruders out, as well as to prevent your dog from roaming. The wire should be at least 40 inches high as many dogs can jump; a return (wire fastened at an angle to the perpendicular) on the top is a good idea. The gate should be fastened with a spring hook or hasp which will not be unfastened by mischance.

If your dog sleeps indoors, he should have his own place, and not be allowed to climb all over the furniture. He should sleep out of drafts, but not right next to the heat, which would make him too sensitive to the cold when he goes outside. If your youngster wants him to sleep on his bed, that is all right, too, but the puppy must learn the difference between his bed and other furniture. Your puppy may sleep in a box big enough to curl up in, or a dog bed or basket, a regulation dog crate, or one made from a packing box with bedding for comfort.

You have already decided where the puppy will sleep before you bring him home. Let him stay there, or in the corner he will soon learn is "his," most of the time, so that he will gain a sense of security from the familiar. Give the puppy a little milk with bread or kibble in it when he arrives, but don't worry if he isn't hungry at first. He will soon develop an appetite when he grows accustomed to his surroundings. The first night the puppy may cry a bit from lonesomeness, but if he has an old blanket or rug to curl up in he will be cozy. In winter a hot water bottle will help replace the warmth of his littermates, or the ticking of a clock may provide company.

FEEDING YOUR PUPPY

It is best to use the feeding schedule to which the puppy is accustomed, and stick to it except when you feel you can modify or improve it. You will probably want to feed the puppy on one of the commercially prepared dog foods as a base, flavoring it with table scraps and probably a little meat and fat when you have them. Remember that the dog food companies have prepared their food so that it is a balanced ration in itself, and, indeed, many dogs are raised on dog food alone. If you try to change this balance too much you are likely to upset your pet's digestion, and the dog will not be as well fed in the long run. Either kibble or meal is a good basic food, and the most economical way to feed your dog.

Milk is good for puppies and some grown dogs like it. Big bones are fine to chew on, especially for teething puppies, but small bones such as chicken, chop or fish bones are always dangerous; they may splinter or stick in the digestive tract. Table scraps such as meat, fat, or vegetables will furnish variety and vitamins, but fried or starchy foods such as potatoes and beans will not be of much food value. Adding a tablespoonful of fat (lard or drippings) to the daily food will keep your puppy's skin healthy and make his coat shine.

Remember that all dogs are individuals. It is the amount that will keep your dog in good health which is right for him, not the "rule-book" amount. A feeding chart to give you some idea of what the average puppy will eat follows:

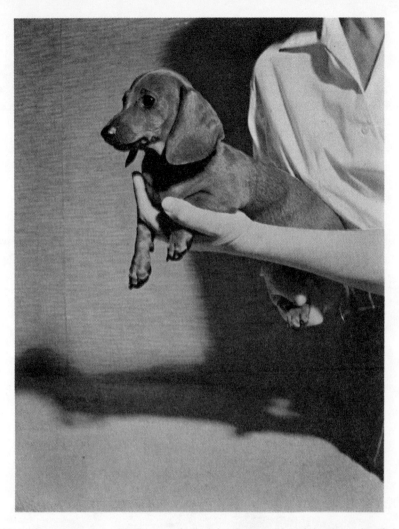

This is the proper way to handle a gentle Dachshund puppy. If Dachshunds are handled roughly, especially when they are young, they may not develop the wonderful personality that has made them so popular.

WEANING TO 3 MONTHS: A.M. ¼ cup dog food (meal or kibble) mixed with warm water. NOON ½ cup milk; cereal, kibble or biscuits. P.M. ¼ cup dog food, ¼ lb. meat or canned dog food, 1 tsp. fat, table scraps. BEDTIME ½ cup milk, biscuit.

3-6 MONTHS: A.M. ½-1 cup dog meal or kibble, mixed. NOON ½ cup milk as above, soft-boiled egg occasionally. P.M. ½-1 cup meal, as above.

6 MONTHS-1 YEAR: A.M. 1½ cups dog meal or 1 cup milk with stale bread, kibble, etc. P.M. 1 cup meal with ¼ lb. meat, scraps, etc.

OVER 1 YEAR: A.M. Half of evening meal if desired. P.M. 2 cups meal, as above.

A Miniature will, of course, eat less than the above amounts, while it is quite likely that any dog will eat more or less than these average figures. Your pup, to be healthy and happy, should be neither too thin nor overweight. However, Dachshunds tend to be overfed and underexercised, so it is better to err, if at all, by underfeeding.

If your Dachshund makes a mistake you can clean the area easily with warm water to which a few drops of vinegar have been added. Scold your Dachshund when he breaks his training.

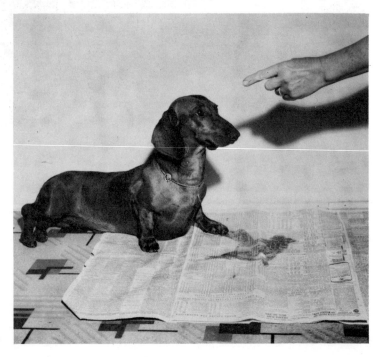

If you cannot take your Dachshund out for relief, provide a corner with some newspaper so your pet can be comfortable. If you use soiled paper for a few days, your Dachshund will be better able to accustom himself to the area.

HOUSEBREAKING YOUR PUPPY

As soon as you get your puppy you can begin to housebreak him but remember that you can't expect too much of him until he is five months old or so. A baby puppy just cannot control himself, so it is best to give him an opportunity to relieve himself before the need arises.

Don't let the puppy wander through the whole house; keep him in one or two rooms under your watchful eye. If he sleeps in the house and has been brought up on newspapers, keep a couple of pages handy on the floor. When he starts to whimper, puts his nose to the ground or runs around looking restless, take him to the paper before an "accident" occurs. After he has behaved, praise him and let him roam again. It is much better to teach him the right way than to punish him for misbehaving. Puppies are naturally clean and can be housebroken easily, given the chance. If a mistake should occur, and mistakes are bound to happen, wash it immediately with tepid water, followed by another rinse with water to which a few drops of vinegar have been added. A dog will return to the same place if there is any odor left, so it is important to remove all traces.

Above: A typical pose taken by a well groomed wire-haired Dachshund. Note the cute whiskers.

Below: This Dachshund is in training for a show. The trainer is using a light lead specially made for show purposes.

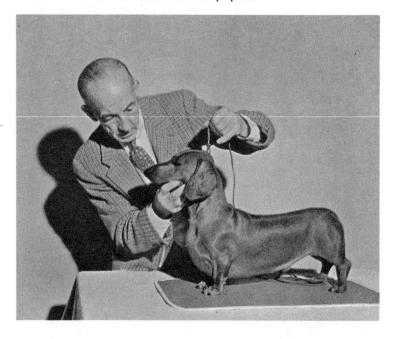

This picture shows why Dachshunds need strong, stubby tails. The German breeders who originated this breed say that they needed strong tails so they could be pulled out of rabbit holes if they got stuck. Here we see two Dachshunds that use their tails, in different ways, to support themselves when they stand up.

If your puppy sleeps outside, housebreaking will be even easier. Remember that the puppy has to relieve himself after meals and whenever he wakes up, as well as sometimes in between. So take him outside as soon as he shows signs of restlessness indoors, and stay with him until he has performed. Then praise and pat him, and bring him back inside as a reward. Since he is used to taking care of himself outdoors, he will not want to misbehave in the house, and will soon let you know when he wants to go out.

You can combine indoor paper training and outdoor housebreaking by taking the puppy out when convenient and keeping newspaper available and within reach at other times; at night if he sleeps indoors while he is a puppy. As he grows older he should be able to control himself for longer periods. If he starts to misbehave, scold him and take him out or to his paper. Punishment after the fact will not accomplish as much as catching the puppy in the act.

The older puppy or grown dog should be able to remain overnight in the house without needing to go out, unless he is ill. If your dog barks or acts restless, take him out once, but unless he relieves himself right away, take him back indoors and shut him in his quarters. No dog will soil his bed if he can avoid it, and your pet will learn to control himself overnight if he has to.

VETERINARY CARE

You will want your puppy to be protected against the most serious puppyhood diseases: distemper and infectious hepatitis. So your first action after getting him will be to take him to your veterinarian for his shots and a check-up, if he has not already received them. He may have had all or part of the immunization as early as two months, so check with the seller before you bring your puppy home.

You may give the puppy temporary serum which provides immunity for about two weeks, but nowadays permanent vaccine providing lifelong immunity can be given so early that the serum is seldom used, except as a precaution in outbreaks. The new vaccine is a combined one against distemper and hepatitis, and may be given in one or three (two weeks apart) shots. Your veterinarian probably has a preferred type, so go along with him, as either method is protective in a very high percentage of cases.

There is now an effective anti-rabies vaccine, which you can give to your dog if there should be an outbreak of this disease in your neighborhood. It is not permanent, however, so unless local regulations demand it, there is little value in giving the vaccine in ordinary circumstances.

WORMING

Your puppy has probably been wormed at least once, since puppies have a way of picking up worms, particularly in a kennel where they are

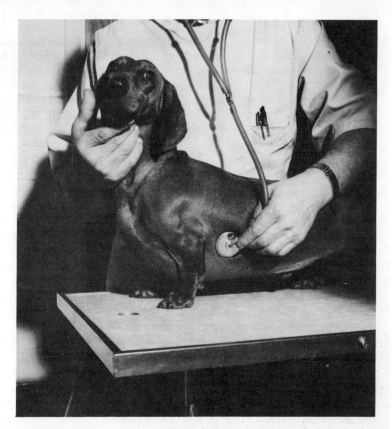

Your veterinarian is your dog's best friend. He understands animals and their illnesses better than anyone else. If your Dachshund becomes ill, have the vet check him over. A periodical physical for every Dachshund is recommended.

exposed to other dogs. Find out when he was last wormed and the date, if any, for re-worming. Older dogs are usually able to throw off worms if they are in good condition when infected, but unless the puppy is given some help when he gets worms, he is likely to become seriously sick. New worm medicines containing the non-toxic but effective piperazines may be bought at your pet store or druggist's, and you can give them yourself. But remember to follow instructions carefully and do not worm the puppy unless you are sure he has worms.

If the puppy passes a long, string-like white worm in his stool or coughs one up, that is sufficient evidence, and you should proceed to worm him. Other indications are: general listlessness, a large belly, dull coat, mattery eye and coughing, but these could also be signs that your puppy is coming down with some disease. If you only *suspect* that he has worms, take him to your veterinarian for a check-up and stool examination before worming.

The standards for the ideal Dachshund head include medium oval eyes, ears that are broad, long, rounded and set high and well back, and a neck that is long and muscular.

Above: A Dachshund puppy makes a fine pet but children must learn to respect their pets and not abuse them. Baby dogs are almost as delicate as human babies.

Below: All varieties of Dachshunds are courageous, intelligent and affectionate.

THE FEMALE PUPPY

If you want to spay your female you can have it done while she is still a puppy. Her first seasonal period will probably occur between eight and ten months, although it may be as early as six or delayed until she is a year old. She may be spayed before or after this, or you may breed her (at a later season) and still spay her afterward.

The first sign of the female's being in season is a thin red discharge, which will increase for about a week, when it changes color to a thin yellowish stain, lasting about another week. Simultaneously there is a swelling of the vulva, the dog's external sexual organ. The second week is the crucial period, when she could be bred if you wanted her to have puppies, but it is possible for the period to be shorter or longer, so it is best not to take unnecessary risks at any time. After a third week the swelling decreases and the period is over for about six months.

If you have an absolutely climb-proof and dig-proof run, within your yard, it will be safe to leave her there, but otherwise the female in season should be shut indoors. Don't leave her out alone for even a minute; she should be exercised only on leash. If you want to prevent the neighborhood dogs from hanging around your doorstep, as they inevitably will as soon as they discover that your female is in season, take her some distance away from the house before you let her relieve herself. Take her to a nearby park or field in the car for a chance to stretch her legs. After the three weeks are up you can let her out as before, with no worry that she can have puppies until the next season. But if you want to have her spayed, consult your veterinarian about the time and age at which he prefers to do it. With a young dog the operation is simple and after a night or two at the animal hospital she can be at home, wearing only a small bandage as a souvenir.

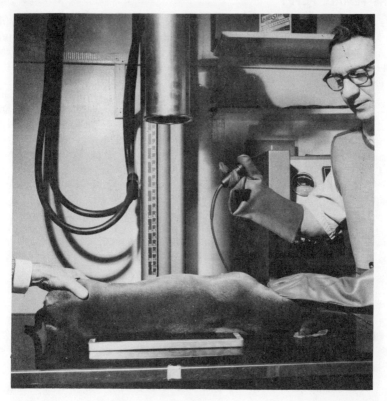

Female Dachshunds can be operated upon so that they can never have puppies. Since your Dachshund should not run about without any attention, there is little chance that she can mate with a stray dog or become involved with another Dachshund. Check with your local veterinary surgeon and he will examine your Dachshund and best advise you.

Above: An ideal long-haired Dachshund. Long-hairs should have a coat similar in texture to that of an Irish Setter. Their main disadvantage is that they get dirty more quickly and they are harder to wash and dry.

Below: Dachshunds must be thoroughly dried after a bath, even in warm weather.

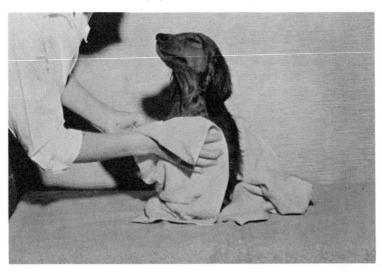

It's amazing how a short-legged dog like a Dachshund can jump onto your favorite chair, but he can! If you once allow your pet Dachshund the freedom of your furniture, it will be a habit that will be extremely difficult to break.

4. Caring for Your Adult Dachshund

When your dog reaches its first birthday it is no longer a puppy, although it will not be fully mature and developed for some months. For all intents and purposes, however, it may be considered full-grown and adult now.

DIET

You may prefer to continue feeding your dog twice a day, although it can now eat all it needs in one daily meal. Usually it is best to feed the one, or main, meal in the evening; most dogs eat better and digest their food better this way. If your dog skips an occasional meal, don't worry; but after half an hour remove the food if it turns up its nose at it, and feed less at the next meal. Otherwise it will develop the habit of picking at the food, and dog food left out too long becomes stale or spoiled.

The best indication of the correct amount to feed your dog is its state of health. A fat dog is not a healthy one; just as with human beings, carrying excess weight strains the heart—and whole body. If you cannot give your dog more exercise, cut down on the food, and remember that those dog biscuits fed as snacks or rewards count as calories. If your dog is thin, increase the food, and add a little extra fat. Add flavoring it likes to pep up appetite. The average grown dog needs two cups of dog meal or half a pound of canned dog food a day, but use your judgment for YOUR dog.

CLEANLINESS AND GROOMING

The Dachshund, with his clean ways, needs little in the way of grooming. From puppyhood he should be accustomed to brushing with a hound glove or soft brush and to having his teeth checked and being handled all over—frequently by you as well as in the veterinarian's semi-annual checkup.

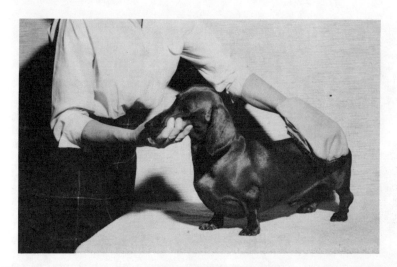

Above: From his early age a Dachshund should be rubbed and brushed. A hound glove will serve this purpose nicely. Brushing removes loose hairs and makes the coat healthier and shinier.

Below: Examine your Dachshund's teeth regularly and remove all foreign particles with a cotton swab.

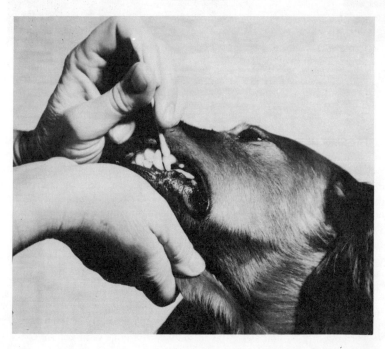

Since a Dachshund is such a short dog, he is difficult for a driver to see. Train your Dachshund to stay away from cars so that no unfortunate accident can deprive you of a wonderful pet.

The Smooth Dachshund particularly needs little care; brushing will help to remove loose, dead hair. The Wire-coat should be fairly even throughout, but longer on whiskers and eyebrows, shorter on the ears. The Long-hair should resemble an Irish Setter, with luxuriant hair on tail, legs and ears, as well as longer hair on the belly. A slight wave is permissible, but the hair should not be noticeably parted down the middle of the back and should never be woolly or bushy. Strip out curly hair on the elbows, and trim between the toes to prevent the thick hair pushing them apart.

To prevent hair from becoming a nuisance, give a vigorous brushing several times a week. This will leave the hair on your grooming brush instead of the furniture. If your dog becomes used to it as a puppy grooming will be enjoyable in later life. Teach your dog to stand still on a table or bench while you are brushing and checking it over; this is good show training as well as being useful for control in other situations.

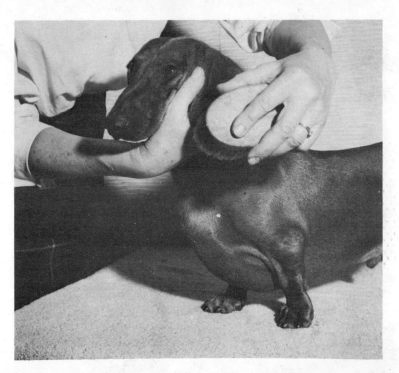

Above: The Smooth Dachshund needs little in the way of bathing, combing and other grooming. Brushing away dirt particles, dead hair and foreign matter is essential to the health of your pet Dachshund. Don't let him down.

Below: If your pet Dachshund doesn't get enough exercise, his toenails may require filing. Take care: *don't file to the vein!*

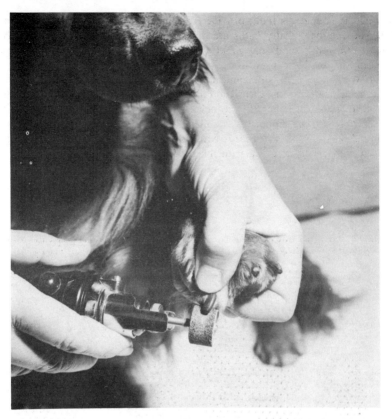

If you are in doubt about your ability to clip or file your Dachshund's nails properly, take him to your veterinarian and have the nails done there.

Toenails, too, will push toes apart, so keep them clipped quite short, and this will also prevent their tearing and hurting your dog. Clipping once a month with toenail or especially designed clippers available in pet shops will keep them under control. Never take off too much at one time or risk cutting into the "quick," which is sensitive and will bleed. Cut just the tip and then round off with a file, if you want to shorten the nails. Cutting will make the quick recede gradually.

Your Dachshund will seldom need a bath unless it gets into something smelly or is unusually dirty. Too much bathing dries the skin and causes shedding, so don't overdo it, in any event. If you use soap, be sure to rinse thoroughly so that no residue is left to irritate the skin.

After the bath your dog should be dried thoroughly and kept in a warm place so that it won't suffer a chill. If it begins to smell a little "doggy" it may not be your dog's fault; provide fresh bedding, and it will be a sweeter dog. The commercial dry baths are quick and easy to use. If odor persists, check teeth, tonsils and anal glands; your veterinarian's eye is quicker than yours to see possible causes.

If your dog's skin is dry and dandruffy, or sheds excessively, it may be due to a lack of fat in the diet. Rub olive oil into the skin and add a spoonful of lard to the food. Other skin troubles, shown by redness, scratching, or a sore on the surface, should be examined immediately by your veterinarian. Don't delay, as any skin disease is hard to cure, once it takes hold. If caught early, it will usually clear up with the prescribed treatment.

Special nail clippers are available from your pet supplier. Use them to trim your Dachshund's nails, but cut carefully so the vein which runs through the nail is not damaged.

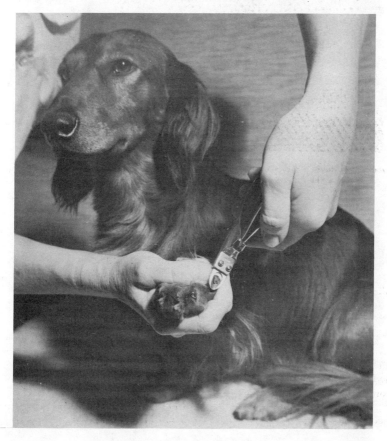

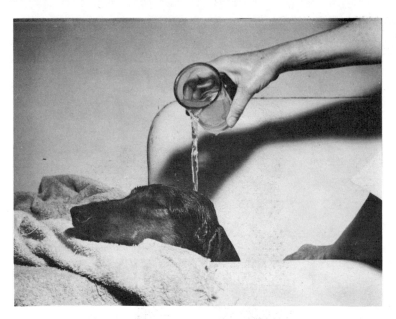

Above: Before lathering your Dachshund, wet him thoroughly by pouring warm water over his head.

Below: Take care not to get soap into his ears or eyes as it is extremely painful and hard to remove.

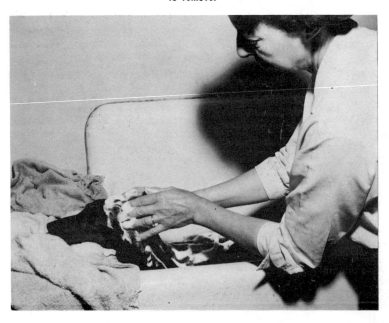

Above: Wrap your Dachshund securely in a heavy bath towel to protect him from chill.

Below: Your Dachshund will shake himself after a bath. Keep him well covered to protect yourself from the spray.

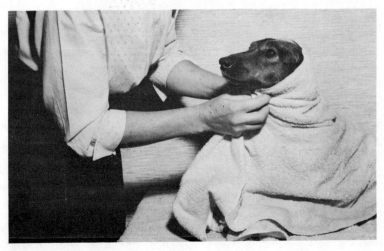

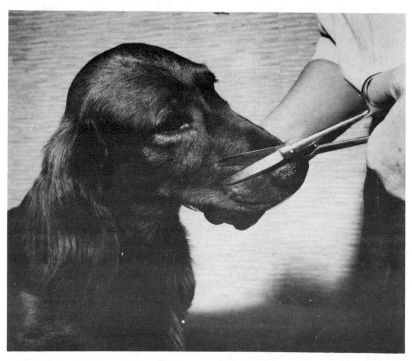

When trimming your Dachshund's face or feet, use blunt-nosed scissors or you might injure the dog if he suddenly moved.

NOSE, TEETH, EARS AND EYES

Normally a dog's nose, teeth, ears and eyes need no special care. The dog's nose is cool and moist to the touch (unless he has been in a warm house); however, the "cold nose" theory is only a partial indication of health or sickness. A fever, for instance, would be shown by a hot, dry nose, but other illness might not cause this. The dog's eyes are normally bright and alert, with the eyelid down in the corner, not over the eye. If the haw is bloodshot or partially covers the eye, it may be a sign of illness, or irritation. If your dog has matter in the corners of the eyes, bathe with a mild eye wash; obtain ointment from your veterinarian or pet shop to treat a chronic condition.

If your dog seems to have something wrong with his ears which causes him to scratch at them or shake his head, cautiously probe the ear with a cotton swab. An accumulation of wax will probably work itself out. But dirt or dried blood is indicative of ear mites or infection, and should be treated immediately. Sore ears in the summer, due to fly bites, should be

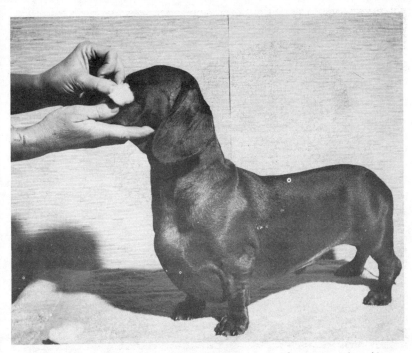

Above: Normally your Dachshund requires little attention. To clean mucus from his eyes use a small piece of cotton.

Below: To clean his ears to prevent mites, use a cotton swab and work carefully.

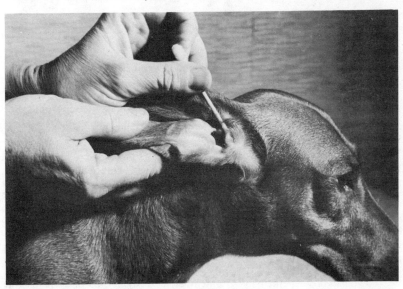

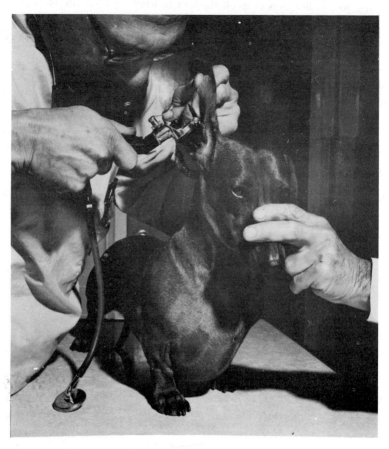

Sometimes a Dachshund may pick up mites in his ear or get ear canker. Though remedies are available to help rid your dog of this pest, it is advisable to have his ears checked by a veterinarian first.

washed with mild soap and water, then covered with a soothing ointment, gauze-wrapped if necessary. Keep the dog protected from insects, inside if necessary, until his ears heal.

The dog's teeth will take care of themselves, although you may want your veterinarian to scrape off the unsightly tartar accumulation occasionally. A good hard bone will help to do the same thing.

PARASITES

Should your dog pick up fleas or other skin parasites from neighbors' dogs or from the ground, weekly use of a good DDT- or Chlordane-base flea powder will keep them off. Remember to dust his bed and change the bedding, too, as flea eggs drop off the host to hatch and wait in likely places for the dog to return. In warm weather a weekly dusting or monthly dip is good prevention.

If your grown dog is well fed and in good health you will probably have no trouble with worms. He may pick them up from other dogs, however, so if you suspect worms, have a stool examination made and, if necessary, worm him. Fleas, too, are carriers of tapeworm, so that is one good reason to make sure the dog is free from these insects. Roundworms, the dog's most common intestinal parasite, have a life cycle which permits complete eradication by worming twice, ten days apart. The first worming will remove all adults and the second will destroy all subsequently hatched eggs before they in turn can produce more parasites.

When rubbing flea powder into your Dachshund's coat be sure to get the hair under the neck. Hold your dog's head up this way and rub the powder in thoroughly.

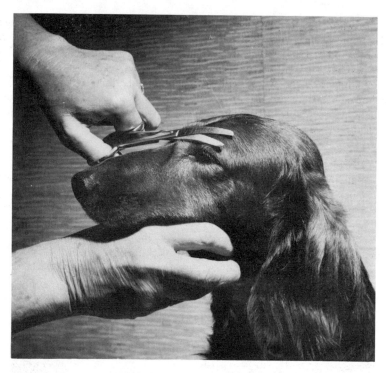

Special flat-curved scissors with blunt ends are available to trim off hairs that stick out and mar the Dachshund's elegant profile.

FIRST AID

Should your dog be injured, you can give him first aid which is, in general, similar to that for a human. The same principles apply. Superficial wounds should be disinfected and healing ointment applied. If the cut is likely to get dirty apply a bandage and restrain the dog so that he won't keep trying to remove it. A cardboard ruff will prevent him from licking his chest or body. Nails can be taped down to prevent scratching.

A board splint should be put on before moving a dog which might have a broken bone. If you are afraid that the dog will bite from pain, use a bandage muzzle made from a long strip of cloth, wrapped around the muzzle, then tied under the jaw and brought up behind the ears to hold it on. In case of severe bleeding apply a tourniquet—a strip of cloth wrapped around a stick to tighten it will do—between the cut on a limb and the heart, but loosen it every few minutes to avoid damaging the circulation.

If you suspect that your dog has swallowed poison, try to get him to vomit by giving him salt water or mustard in water. In all these cases, rush him to your veterinarian as soon as possible, after alerting him by phone.

In warm weather the most important thing to remember for your dog's sake is providing fresh water. If he tends to slobber and drink too much, it may be offered at intervals of an hour or so instead of being available at all times, but it should be fresh and cool. Don't over-exercise the dog or let the children play too wildly with him in the heat of the day. Don't leave him outside without shade, and never leave a dog in a car which could become overheated in the sun. It should always have some shade and ventilation through the windows.

THE OLD DOG

With the increased knowledge and care available, there is no reason why your dog should not live to a good old age. As he grows older he may need a little additional care, however. Remember that a fat dog is not healthy, particularly as he grows older, and limit his food accordingly. The older dog needs exercise as much as ever, although his heart cannot bear the strain of sudden and violent exertion. His digestion may not be as good as it was as a puppy, so follow your veterinarian's advice about special feeding, if necessary. Failing eyesight or hearing mean lessened awareness of dangers, so you must protect him more than before. The old dog is used to his home,

As your Dachshund get older he may fall victim to ailments. Often your vet will prescribe pills. Hold your dog's head this way, with the skin over his teeth, so he won't snap at you when you shove the pill down his throat.

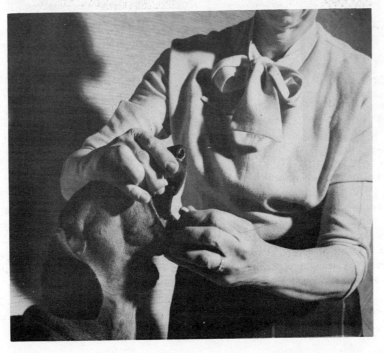

and to set ways, so too many strangers are bound to be a strain. For the same reason, boarding him out or a trip to the vet's are to be avoided unless absolutely necessary.

Should you decide at this time to get a puppy, to avoid being without a dog when your old retainer is no longer with you, be very careful how you introduce the puppy. He is naturally playful and will expect the older dog to respond to his advances. Sometimes the old dog will get a new lease on life from a pup. But don't make him jealous by giving to the newcomer the attention that formerly was exclusively his. Feed them apart, and show the old dog that you still love him the most; the puppy, not being used to individual attention will not mind sharing your love.

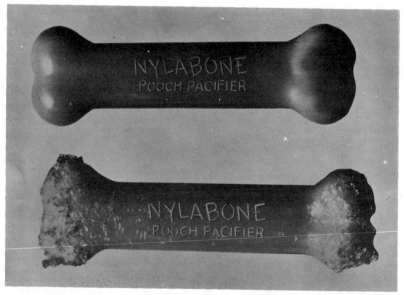

NYLABONE® is a necessity that is available at your local petshop (not in supermarkets). The puppy or grown dog chews the hambone flavored nylon into a frilly dog toothbrush, massaging his gums and cleaning his teeth as he plays. Veterinarians highly recommend this product . . . but beware of cheap imitations which might splinter or break.

5. How to Train Your Dachshund

The Dachshund is a breed easily trained. However, it will take some effort on your part. You cannot expect a dog to be perfectly behaved by instinct any more than you would expect children to be. Most badly behaved dogs are the fault of lack of attention and discipline on the part of their owners; it is up to YOU to make your dog a pleasure to own and not a nuisance to the neighborhood.

You can easily train your dog to become a well-behaved member of your family. Training should begin the day you get him. Although a puppy under six months is too young to expect much in the way of obedience, you should teach him to respect your authority. Be consistent. Don't allow the pup to jump all over you when you are wearing old clothes, because you can't expect him to know the difference when you are dressed for a party. Don't encourage the dog to climb into your lap or onto your bed, then punish him for leaving hair on furniture when you aren't around. Although six months to a year is the best time to begin serious training, a dog of any age can learn if taught with consideration and patience. You *can* teach an old dog new tricks.

Housebreaking has already been covered. You cannot expect perfection from a puppy, or even an older dog, particularly if he is not used to living in a house. Going into a strange place, a dog is likely to be ill at ease and make a mistake for that reason. Remember that once it has happened, the only way to prevent further accidents is to avoid the opportunity and to be sure to remove traces which would remind the dog of previous errors.

After rinsing with warm water, pour a little diluted vinegar on the spot. This will help to remove any trace of odor attracting your dog or others in the future.

Once you have taught your puppy to be clean indoors, and then to use one place outside, you may have some difficulty teaching him to relieve himself when you wish and not just in the accustomed place. Take him out

Dachshunds, like most other dogs, shed dead hairs wherever they lie. If you don't want hairs all over your clothes, keep your Dachshund off the furniture. A Dachshund will usually shed more hair as he gets older and as the weather gets warmer.

as usual when he needs to go, but take him to different places. "Curb your dog" is the law in most cities, and for the sake of others you should train your dog to obey it. It is a convenience when traveling to be able to take your dog on leash to relieve himself, so take the time to teach him before you start off.

COLLAR AND LEASH

Your puppy should become used to a leash and collar at an early age. A leather collar will be outgrown several times before he is full-grown, so buy one for use, not a fancy one for looks. In any case, buy a lightweight collar which will annoy the puppy no more than necessary, and a leather leash with a strong swivel clip on the end. A choke collar made of chrome links or leather is used for training, but never leave it on the dog when he is loose, as it could catch on something and choke him.

Let the puppy wear his collar around until he is used to its feel and weight. After several short periods he will not be distracted by the strangeness and you can attach the leash. Let him pull it around and then try to lead him a bit. He will probably resist, bucking and balking, or simply sit down and refuse to budge. Fight him for a few minutes, dragging him along if necessary, but then let him relax for the day, with plenty of affection and praise. He won't be lead-broken until he learns that he must obey the pull under any circumstance, but don't try to do it in one lesson. Ten minutes a day is long enough for any training. The dog's period of concentration is short and, like a child, he will become bored if you carry it on too long.

TRAINING YOUR DOG TO WALK PROPERLY

Once the puppy has learned his first two lessons, to obey the leash and the word "NO," half your training has been accomplished—you are the master. "Heeling" is a necessity for a well-behaved dog, so teach him to walk beside you, head alongside your leg at the knee. Nothing looks more foolish than a twenty-pound Dachshund pulling his helpless owner along, and it can be annoying to passers-by and other dog owners to have such a dog, however friendly, bear down on them and entangle dogs, people and packages.

Start off walking briskly, with the dog at your left side, giving the command "Heel!" in a firm voice. Pull back with a sharp jerk if he lunges ahead, and if he lags repeat the command and tug the leash, not allowing him to hang back behind you.

REWARD

With all your training give the dog plenty of praise when he obeys; reward is even more important than punishment. A pat on the head and kind word will mean more than tangible rewards to your dog. Do not bribe him with dog candy or treats, as these would come to be more important to the puppy than the command, if repeated. The *time* to train is important, too. A quiet time during the day is ideal, but you can work indoors during the evening, if that is the only time available. At first it is particularly desirable to eliminate all other distractions that might take the puppy's attention off the business at hand. Later on you will wish to accustom him to strange noises and to behaving in an unfamiliar place.

TEACHING YOUR DOG TO COME

After the dog has learned to heel at all speeds on the leash, you can remove the leash and practice heeling free, but have it ready to snap on

again as soon as he begins to lag or wander. Don't take him off leash to show off in strange places where something might frighten him. Obedience without a lead is desirable in case you need it in an emergency.

When the dog understands the pull of the leash he should learn to come. Never call him to you for punishment, or he will be quick to disobey. (Always go to him if he has been disobedient.) To teach him to come, let him reach the end of a long lead, then give the command, pulling him toward you at the same time. As soon as he associates the word "Come" with the action, pull only when he does not respond immediately. As he starts to come, back up to make him learn that he must come from a distance as well as when he is close to you. Soon you can practice without a leash, but if he is slow to come or actively disobedient, go to him and pull him toward you, repeating the command. More practice with leash on is needed.

Teach your Dachshund to sit and lie down so that you can be comfortable when you happen to meet someone on the street while you are walking your dog. Too often the dog takes the master for the walk and not vice versa.

TEACHING YOUR DOG TO SIT AND STAY

"Sit," "Down," and "Stay" are among the most useful commands and will make it easier for you to control your dog on many occasions—when grooming him, when he needs veterinary care, out walking if you meet a strange dog, or in the car, to mention a few. Teaching him to sit is the first step. With collar and leash on have him stand in the "Heel" position. Give the command, "Sit," at the same time pulling up on the leash in your right hand and pressing down on his hindquarters with your left. As soon as he sits, release the pressure and praise him.

To teach your dog to stay, bring your hand close to his face with a direct motion, at the same time as you give the order. Ask him to remain only a few seconds at first, but gradually the time can be increased and you can leave him at a distance. If he should move, return immediately and make him sit and stay again, after scolding him.

To teach your dog to lie down, have him sit facing you. Pull down on the leash by putting your foot on it and pulling at the same time as you say "Down." Gesture toward the ground with a sweep of your arm. When he begins to understand what is wanted, do it without the leash and alternate voice and hand signals. Teach him to lie down from standing as well as sitting position, and begin to do it from a distance. Hand signals are particularly useful when your dog can see you but is too far away to hear, and they may be used in teaching all commands.

If you are consistent and curb your puppy every time he misbehaves, he is not likely to acquire bad habits. Every pup goes through teething, but if he has a bone or toy he is less likely to chew the furniture. Teach him to stay off furniture and not to jump up, so he won't do it later. If you call him back or jerk on his leash when he wants to chase a car or bicycle, he'll soon learn it is not permitted.

With a dog which has bad habits already, sterner measures are needed. Chasing cars can be cured with a sharpshooter's water pistol, or a whole bucket of water dumped from behind when he doesn't expect it. Prevention is the easiest method.

To teach your Dachshund to stay, hold your hand close to his face with a very direct motion and give the verbal command "stay" at the same time. This simultaneous physical and verbal command is extremely important.

Training your Dachshund for field work is very rewarding. A Dachshund loves to work out in the open and his natural hunting instincts make him a fine rabbit dog.

Since a Dachshund is such an intelligent dog, you won't have too much trouble training him to do tricks. This long-haired fellow is "begging." His mistress is very proud of him, too. You can be proud of your dog if he is well trained. *It's all up to you!*

TRICKS

Most dogs develop their own little tricks which you can show off to your friends. Dachshunds are naturals at sitting up, with their build, so can easily be coaxed up from a sitting position. Hold the pup up at the same time as you repeat "Up" or "Beg," and then praise and release him. You can teach him to shake hands by repeatedly taking hold of his paw and saying "Give me your paw," "Shake hands," or whatever you wish him to respond too. Remember that all commands must be the same each time if you want your dog to obey; he has a limited vocabulary and will be confused if you give one command one day and a different one the next. You can teach your dog to roll over by making him go through the motions from a lying-down position, to fetch, and to perform many other tricks. Always remember to give commands in the simplest way, and to praise him when he obeys.

6. Caring for the Female and Raising Puppies

Whether or not you bought your female dog intending to breed her, some preparation is necessary when and if you decide to take this step.

WHEN TO BREED

It is usually best to breed on the second or third season. Plan in advance the time of year which is best for you, taking into account where the puppies will be born and raised. You will keep them until they are at least six weeks old, and a litter of husky pups takes up considerable space by then. Other considerations are selling the puppies (Christmas vs. springtime sales), your own vacation, and time available to care for them. You'll need at least an hour a day to feed and clean up after the mother and puppies but probably it will take you much longer—with time out to admire and play with them!

CHOOSING THE STUD

You can plan to breed your female about 6½ months after the start of her last season, although a variation of a month or two either way is not unusual. Choose the stud dog and make arrangements well in advance. If you are breeding for show stock, which may command better prices, a mate should be chosen with an eye to complementing the deficiencies of your female. If possible, they should have several ancestors in common within the last two or three generations, as such combinations generally "click" best. He should have a good show record or be the sire of show winners if old enough to be proven.

The owner of such a male usually charges a fee for the use of the dog of $50 or more. This does not guarantee a litter, but you generally have the right to breed your female again if she does not have puppies. In some cases the owner of the stud will agree to take a choice puppy in place of a stud fee. You should settle all details beforehand, including the possibility of a single surviving puppy, deciding the age at which he is to make his choice and take the pup, and so on.

If you want to raise a litter "just for the fun of it" and plan merely to make use of an available male, the most important selection point is temperament. Make sure the dog is friendly as well as healthy, because a bad disposition could appear in his puppies, and this is the worst of all traits in a dog destined to be a pet. In such cases a "stud fee puppy," not necessarily the choice of the litter, is the usual payment.

PREPARATION FOR BREEDING

Before you breed your female, make sure she is in good health. She should be neither too thin nor too fat. Any skin disease *must* be cured, before it can be passed on to the puppies. If she has worms she should be wormed before being bred or within three weeks afterward. It is generally considered a good idea to revaccinate her against distemper and hepatitis before the puppies are born. This will increase the immunity the puppies receive during their early, most vulnerable period.

The female will probably be ready to breed 12 days after the first colored discharge. You can usually make arrangements to board her with the owner of the male for a few days, to insure her being there at the proper time, or you can take her to be mated and bring her home the same day. If she still appears receptive she may be bred again two days later. However, some females never show signs of willingness, so it helps to have the experience of a breeder. Usually the second day after the discharge changes color is the proper time, and she may be bred for about three days following. For an additional week or so she may have some discharge and attract other dogs by her odor, but can seldom be bred.

THE FEMALE IN WHELP

You can expect the puppies nine weeks from the day of breeding, although 61 days is as common as 63. During this time the female should receive normal care and exercise. If she was overweight, don't increase her food at first; excess weight at whelping time is bad. If she is on the thin side build her up, giving some milk and biscuit at noon if she likes it. You may add one of the mineral and vitamin supplements to her food, to make sure that the puppies will be healthy. As her appetite increases, feed her more. During the last two weeks the puppies grow enormously and she will probably have little room for food and less appetite. She should be tempted with meat, liver and milk, however.

As the female in whelp grows heavier, cut out violent exercise and jumping. Although a dog used to such activities will often play with the children or run around voluntarily, restrain her for her own sake.

PREPARING FOR THE PUPPIES

Prepare a whelping box a few days before the puppies are due, and

When breeding any dog, but especially a Dachshund, be sure that the parents are as fine as possible, with the coat and color you want. Then the puppies will be likely to meet with your approval.

allow the mother to sleep there overnight or to spend some time in it during the day to become accustomed to it. Then she is less likely to try to have her pups under the front porch or in the middle of your bed. A variety of places will serve, such as a corner of your garage (in warm weather), or an unused room or quiet spot. In summer, a large outdoor doghouse will do, if it is well protected from rain and draft, although it will be harder for you to clean, and to inspect the puppies. A whelping box serves to separate mother and puppies from visitors and other distractions. The walls should be high enough to keep puppies in and draft-free, yet allow the mother to get away after she has fed the puppies. Three feet square is minimum size, and six-inch walls will keep pups in until they begin to climb, when the sides should be built up. Then the puppies will really need more room anyway, so a double space with one-inch partition down the middle will suit them. You will find them housebreaking themselves surprisingly fast.

Layers of newspaper spread over the whole area will make excellent bedding and be absorbent enough to keep the surface warm and dry. They should be removed daily and replaced with another thick layer. An old quilt or washable blanket makes better footing for the nursing puppies than slippery newspaper during the first week, and is softer for the mother.

Be prepared for the actual whelping several days in advance. Usually the female will tear up papers, refuse food and generally act restless. These may be false alarms; the real test is her temperature, which will drop to below 100° about 12 hours before whelping. Take it with a rectal thermometer morning and evening, and put her in the pen, looking in on her frequently, when the temperature goes down.

WHELPING

Usually little help is needed but it is wise to stay close to make sure that the mother's lack of experience does not cause an unnecessary accident. Be ready to help when the first puppy arrives, for it could smother if she does not break the membrane enclosing it. She should start right away to lick the puppy, drying and stimulating it, but you can do it with a soft rough towel, instead. The afterbirth should follow the birth of each puppy, attached to the puppy by the long umbilical cord. Watch to make sure that each is expelled, anyway, for retaining this material can cause infection. In her instinct for cleanliness the mother will probably eat the afterbirth after biting the cord. One or two will not hurt her; they stimulate milk supply as well as labor for remaining pups. But too many can make her lose appetite for the food she needs to feed her pups and regain her strength. So remove the rest of them along with the wet newspapers and keep the pen dry and clean to relieve her anxiety.

If the mother does not bite the cord, or does it too close to the body, take over the job, to prevent an umbilical hernia. Tearing is recommended, but you can cut it, about two inches from the body, with a sawing motion of scissors, sterilized in alcohol. Then dip the end in a shallow dish of iodine; the cord will dry up and fall off in a few days.

The puppies should follow each other at intervals of not more than half an hour. If more time goes past and you are sure there are still pups to come, a brisk walk outside may start labor again. If she is actively straining without producing a puppy it may be presented backward, a so-called "breach" or upside down birth. Careful assistance with a well-soaped finger to feel for the puppy or ease it back may help, but never attempt to pull it by force against the mother. This could cause serious damage, so let an expert handle it.

If anything seems wrong, waste no time in calling your veterinarian. who can examine her and if necessary give hormones which will bring the remaining puppies. You may want his experience in whelping the litter even if all goes well. He will probably prefer to have the puppies born at his

Your female Dachshund should have her own bed and be made comfortable before the times comes for her to have her puppies. Be prepared for the whelping and if your Dachshund acts a little peculiar, not eating or tearing up her bed, understand that she is acting out of instinct.

hospital rather than to get up in the middle of the night to come to your home. The mother would, no doubt, prefer to stay at home, but you can be sure she will get the best of care in his hospital. If the puppies are born at home and all goes as it should, watch the mother carefully afterward.

It is wise to have the veterinarian check her and the pups.

WEANING THE PUPPIES

Hold each puppy to a breast as soon as he is dry, for a good meal without competition. Then he may join his littermates in the basket, out of his mother's way while she is whelping. Keep a supply of evaporated milk on hand for emergencies, or later weaning. A formula of evaporated milk, corn syrup and a little water with egg yolk should be warmed and fed in a doll or baby bottle if necessary. A supplementary feeding often helps weak pups over the hump. Keep track of birth weights, and weekly readings, thereafter; it will furnish an accurate record of the pups' growth and health.

After the puppies have arrived, take the mother outside for a walk and drink, and then leave her to take care of them. She will probably not want to stay away more than a minute or two for the first few weeks. Be sure to keep water available at all times, and feed her milk or broth frequently, as she needs liquids to produce milk. Encourage her to eat, with her favorite foods, until she asks for it of her own accord. She will soon develop a ravenous appetite and should have at least two large meals a day, with dry food available in addition.

Prepare a warm place to put the puppies after they are born to keep them dry and help them to a good start in life. An electric heating pad or hot water bottle covered with flannel in the bottom of a cardboard box should be set near the mother so that she can see her puppies. She will usually allow you to help, but don't take the puppies out of sight, and let her handle things if your interference seems to make her nervous.

Be sure that all the puppies are getting enough to eat. If the mother, sits or stands, instead of lying still to nurse, the probable cause is scratching from the puppies' nails. You can remedy this by clipping them, as you do hers. Manicure scissors will do for these tiny claws. Some breeders advise disposing of the smaller or weaker pups in a large litter, as the mother has trouble in handling more than six or seven. But you can help her out by preparing an extra puppy box or basket. Leave half the litter with the mother and the other half in a warm place, changing off at two hour intervals at first. Later you may change them less frequently, leaving them all together except during the day. Try supplementary feeding, too; as soon as their eyes open, at about two weeks, they will lap from a dish, anyway.

The puppies should normally be completely weaned at five weeks, although you start to feed them at three weeks. They will find it easier to lap semi-solid food than to drink milk at first, so mix baby cereal with whole or evaporated milk, warmed to body temperature, and offer it to the puppies one at a time, in a saucer. Hold at chin level and stick their noses in, but don't force-feed. A damp sponge afterward prevents most of the food from sticking to the skin, and mother will also help clean them up. Soon broth or babies' meat may be alternated with milk, and you can start them on finely chopped meat. At four weeks they should be eating four meals a day and soon do without their mother entirely. Start on dog meal, gradually adding it to the cereal, and mix it to porridge consistency.

Do not leave water with the puppies at this age; they will use it as a wading pool. They will drink all they need if it is offered several times a day after meals.

As the puppies grow up the mother will go into the pen only to nurse them, first sitting up and then standing. To dry her up completely, keep the mother away for longer periods; after a few days of part-time nursing she can stay away for longer periods, and then completely. The little milk left will be resorbed.

AIRING THE PUPPIES

The puppies may be put outside, unless it is too cold, as soon as their eyes are open, and will benefit from the sunlight and vitamins. A rubber mat or newspapers underneath will protect them from cold or damp. At six weeks they can go outside permanently unless it is very cold, but make sure that they go into their shelter at night or in bad weather. By now cleaning up is a man-sized job, so put them out at least during the day and make your task easier. Be sure to clean their run daily, as worms and other infections are lurking. You can expect the pups to need at least one worming before they are ready to go to new homes, so take a stool sample to your veterinarian before they are three weeks old. If one puppy has worms all should be wormed. Follow the veterinarian's advice, and this applies also to vaccination. If you plan to keep a pup you will want to vaccinate him at the earliest age, so his littermates should be done at the same time.

7. Showing Your Dachshund

As your puppy grows he will doubtless have many admirers among your friends, some of whom are bound to say, "Oh, what a handsome dog —you should certainly show him!" Perhaps even a breeder or judge will say he has show possibilities, and although you didn't buy him with that thought in mind, "Cinderella" champions do come along now and then— often enough to keep dog breeders perennially optimistic.

If you do have ideas of showing your dog, get the opinion of someone with experience first. With favorable criticism, go ahead making plans to show him. For the novice dog and handler, sanction shows are a good way to gain ring poise and experience. These are small shows often held by the local kennel club or breed specialty club, found in many cities. Entry fees are low and paid at the door, breeds and sexes are usually judged together, and the prizes and ribbons are not important. They provide a good opportunity to learn what goes on at a show, and to conquer ring nervousness. Matches are usually held during the evening or on a week-end afternoon, and you need stay only to be judged.

Before you go to a show your dog should be trained—to gait at a trot beside you, with head up and in a straight line. In the ring you will have to gait around the edge with other dogs and then individually up and down the center runner. In addition the dog must stand for examination by the judge, who will look at him closely and feel his head and body structure. He should be taught to stand squarely, hind feet slightly back, head up on the alert. He must hold the pose when you place his feet and show animation for a piece of boiled liver in your hand or a toy mouse thrown in front of you.

ADVANCE PREPARATION

Showing requires practice training sessions in advance; get a friend to act as judge and set the dog up and "show" him for a few minutes every day. If he knows the command "Stay" he should obey and pose as desired, on a low bench or table, as well as on the floor.

Keep your dog's nails trimmed, and the day before the show trim any unkempt hairs which would mar the outline on your Wire or Long-hair. A little hairdressing or oil rubbed into the Smooth coat after vigorous brushing

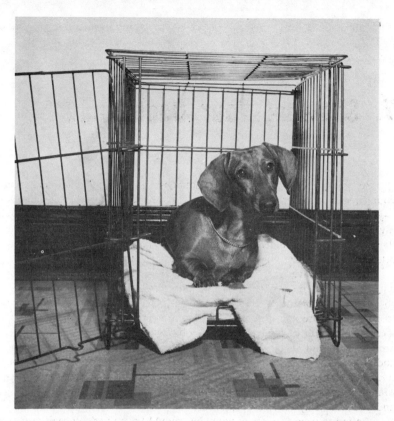
This is one type of cage and bed used in shows for small dogs. This Dachshund seems to be pretty much at home here. If you are planning to show one of your Dachshunds at a competition that requires the presence of your dog overnight, a cage like this is a necessity.

will give it extra gloss, but rub off excess with a cloth. Pack your kit with water (so you won't have to go looking for it and a change of water cannot throw off his digestion), a lightweight show lead and collar combined, and a heavier one and collar to fasten him to the bench where he will remain when not in the exercise ring or being shown.

You will also have to hand in the required identification card at the entrance. This is sent to you in advance by the superintendent along with a timetable of judging, telling you at what hour Dachshunds will be judged, and when you must be in the show building.

SHOW DAY

Don't feed more than a light meal the morning of the show, so that your dog will be comfortable in the car, and will show more enthusiastically.

If he is accustomed to the scent and flavor of boiled liver before the show he will look animated for it held in your hand; otherwise his favorite toy or ball can be carried into the ring with you.

You have probably entered your Dachshund in the puppy (if between six and twelve months) or novice class, which is open to dogs which have not previously won a blue ribbon.

These are the first classes judged, and are followed by bred by exhibitor (owned and bred by the same person), American-bred (whelped in the United States) and Open, which may be divided by color as well as for Standard and Miniature. The first prize winners in each class compete for Winners Dog, to which are awarded a number of points, with a maximum of five, according to a scale on the number of dogs present. The female classes follow on the same order, and then Winners Bitch is judged, and she also receives points, fifteen of which are required to complete the championship.

The Best of (these two) Winners competes against any champions entered for Specials Only for Best of Variety, with the same procedure throughout for Smooth, Long-haired and Wire-haired Dachshunds. All three best of variety winners compete against the other Hound winners: Beagles, Basenjis, Wolfhounds, etc., for Winner of the Hound Group, who goes up against the first place in Sporting, Working, Terrier, Toy and Non-Sporting Groups for the ultimate prize, Best in Show.

There are also obedience trials, in which dogs are judged on performance of certain commands, in increasing difficulty through the series of classes and degrees awarded: Novice—Companion Dog (C.D.); Open—C.D.X. (Excellent) and Utility (U.D.). Requirements for novice can be met by any well-trained house dog, with a little special preparation in an obedience class for the show routine: this includes a stand for examination, long sit, with handler at opposite side of the ring for one minute, and heeling, coming when called. These classes are interesting to watch, and even more interesting for the active participant.